*Inspirational Quotes
From The Doctor*

Lolana Mack Publishing: All rights reserved. Without limiting the rights under copyright reserved above. No part of this publication may be reproduced, stored in or introduced into a retrieval system, or transmitted, in any form, or by any means (electronic, mechanical, photocopying, recording or otherwise), without the prior written permission from both the author and publisher Lolana Mack Publishing, except brief quotes used in reviews.

©2019 by Lolana Mack Publishing:
lolanamackpublishing@gmail.com
ISBN: 978-0-9977804-5-1

Cover Design: Janiel Escueta

Format: CWP

Dedication

Dedicated to my DAD - Rev Dr. Samuel Kilo Kengwa, who passed away January 2015. The Graveyard is rich with our loved ones.

To my children Geomar and Reglice Ngwang; you inspire me to be great. Love you both.

To my Husband George Ngwang; we are going through this journey of Faith. Thanks for the love and support.

Inspirational Quotes From The Doctor

"Life is full of surprises and challenges but stand firm to yourself and beliefs. You will come out on top."

"When life takes you down the valley, listen and learn; so when you climb you will have bullets to sustain the uncertainties life throws at you."

"Failing is necessary for an individual to grow."

So learn from your mistakes and be great.

"Success comes with a price of failing."

Without failures you will not know how to climb a ladder of success.

"To succeed you must learn to take risks
and open your faith."

"Listen to your inner you

Trust you

Build you

Uplift you

The YOU is essential."

"Never let anyone tell you it's impossible;

Follow your dream and

work hard at it.

Impossibilities will be possibilities someday

as long as you keep on trying."

"Love all

Love you

Love the uncertainties

It will build you."

"There is no marriage without problems. Run away from friends who say they have no problem in their marriage. Those problems make you strong and that is how you celebrate anniversaries."

"Marriage is a job;

Work on it DAILY

Pray on it DAILY

Discuss with your partner DAILY."

It will take shape.

"Never lose yourself in a marriage.

Build you first

Love you first

Then you are able to give and work on the marriage".

"People are Divorced in a marriage in their mind and soul even though they are still married on paper. Work on you and build a better you. Then marriage becomes a safe place."

"Anyone you call a friend should be a blessing to you, able to add success and build you up. Disconnect from friends who always bring the negative in life."

"As you climb up the ladder of life

treat people with dignity and respect;

Because as you go down the ladder of life

Someone will catch you, preventing you

from falling flat on your face."

"Respect is earned

Respect is given

Respect is reciprocal

Respect is an art of life

Respect is pure

Respect is genuine

Respect is faith."

"Pay yourself with love

Pay yourself with respect

Pay yourself with truth

Pay yourself with honesty

Life is worth living."

"Pray for your kids

Pray for yourself

Pray for your spouse

Pray for your enemies

Love is a peaceful and gentle word."

Share with people…

"When your friends doubt, you pray

Your spouse doubts, you pray

Your enemies doubt, you pray

Never prove anything to anyone

Only prove to yourself."

"Never defend yourself with your mouth,

Let your job speak on its own."

"Your spouse will fail you

Your friends will fail you

Your children will fail you

Then, you will find you."

"In any conflict silence is the winner."

"Be at peace with you,

there is no greater joy

than loving you."

"The graveyard is very rich. Everyone must go through the graveyard, so confront your fears and enjoy the journey."

"Death is inevitable.

No one is privileged and

All on earth will take the same path;

Live your life to the best of your ability."

"Never judge anyone.

Life is full of challenges and

all have different ways of dealing with life.

No one is perfect."

"Faith is believing without knowing the outcome."

"Biblical"

"Stay cool!

Life is a journey like a roller coaster.

The roller coaster does come to an end."

"Love is pure,

Love is giving even without receiving,

Love brings peace."

"Keep on believing in yourself.

Nobody can keep you away from your dreams.

Extend yourself."

"Choose your words wisely and do not let emotions take you over. At times, silence is the answer."

"Loving you is the best gift to yourself."

"Kids are a gift. Kids will give you joy and sadness. But the greatest gift is the satisfaction of love you gain from having them."

"The joy of having children is heavenly; The best moments in life."

"Money is good.

Money will buy lots of earthly things.

However, money should not

overtake the person

Because being human is

better than money."

"Friends are a gift.

You will find your true friends

in times of need and trouble."

"Your best friend is yourself.

No one can love you better than you."

"Don't' let anyone tell you

'You can't do it'

Follow your dreams,

Be determined,

Dedicate yourself to what you believe in."

"People will say you can't.

Be persistent with your work;

You will have failures and

You will have wins

The best is all within you."

"Why worry?

Life is unpredictable.

Follow your path,

accept your weaknesses and strengths;

This makes you stronger."

"We need to work to provide

for our families.

Believing and trusting in God is how

we maintain our livelihood."

"Your loved ones will betray you,

Your loved ones will talk about you,

But it's because of insecurities.

Always trust your heart to forgive."

"Challenges will come your way. It's how you handle those issues that will determine your future."

"Always look forward;

Let your life be a reflection of you.

Life is a journey."

"Focus on your results as the

journey will have

turbulence, which is

expected to perfect you along the way."

"Commitment is Important in life;

To your spouse

Your kids

Your job

Yourself."

"Love who you are.

Nobody makes you happy;

Only you can make you happy."

"If you think you will fail before starting, then you have."

Think positive in all you do/ by trusting your inner self.

"Jump before you think with any project, because over-thinking is crippling and distasteful."

"Failure is the best experience ever. If you don't fail you might not be able to handle obstacles along the way."

"Stay away from negative friends.

Stay away from negative thoughts.

Staying positive is the only way."

"Success is within you."

Do not look anywhere else, if you do you are short citing yourself.

"Vacation is good for the soul, mind, body and spirit. Take a vacation no matter how short/long or the cost."

"Keep moving no matter how rough the road is. The end matters and the in-between will strengthen you."

"Follow your dreams. Only you can turn on and off the lights."

Only you matter/ no one else matters.

"Embrace life and make it circle around you."
Only you have the power to be great.
Look ahead, looking behind will distract you.

"Life is full of changes so

Make adjustments as it occurs.

Those changes will serve you and your life

to attain inner peace And arrive

at your goals."

"Faith has strengthened me to confront my inner feelings, which have made me reach for stars."

"Strive for success.
Work outside your norm.
When you feel uncomfortable,
you are on the right path and
success is near."

"Work into yourself and center your

dreams. It's all within you."

The 'you' is the most powerful tool, never

lose sight of it.

"In life there are negatives and positives, pick your battles and move forward." Do not dwell in the past, keep moving forward and you will succeed.

"To succeed in business, you have to be

dedicated to you.

Determine your goals and

Depend on your inner self."

"As you climb the ladder of success,
the failures that you have will help you
brace the fall and
overcome challenges along the way."

"Live life to the fullest
until you satisfy your whole self and
magnify your talent without fears."

"Strive for your dreams with all of YOU.

It's only YOU that can do it."

YOU is the most powerful asset. Build YOU!

"I love being a Physician;

Loving my inner self and

Loving all of me

has strengthened me

to develop a more satisfied self."

"Life is always changing.

Love, happiness, and success is a choice in

my life."

"Listen to your inner thoughts;
They take you to your destiny faster than
individuals."

"God is faithful.

Only trust HIM, with all of you."

"Follow the footsteps of the word and your path will be blessed."

"Love life

Love people

Love you

Love all."

Be true to yourself and you will make an

impact.

"Life is beautiful

Life is change forever.

Life is a path; it can be slippery or straight.

Walk on it gently and listen to the

whispers."

"Make the impossible possible when you try your best."

The impossible can only be done by YOU. Self/YOU is very powerful. Keep that in mind.

"Dedicated to yourself

Determined to yourself

Dependable to self."

All will fall into place to lead you to success.

"We need challenges to succeed;
We need challenges to re-route our GPS."
Life will re-route you and you need to be flexible to survive.

"Always the best."

Is the only way.

"Listen to your inner self to refresh your body and soul."

Always stay positive no matter the circumstances.

Positivity heals the body and puts your enemies at a distance.

"Marriage is not perfect, but it is beautiful. Marriage is a job, but it is beautiful. Marriage is very challenging, but it is beautiful."

"Children are gifts from God.
Parenting comes with challenges;
Good and bad.
Embrace it and
enjoy God's beautiful creations."

"My life is not all sugar and

Not all bitter.

My life is a mixture of both,

which have made me whole."

"Life is a journey of ups and downs.

Downs open your eyes and

give you strength,

ups make you appreciate the journey."

"Friends are good

Friends are envious at times

Friends will gossip

Friends at times want to see you down

But with challenges and experiences, you will know

Who your friends are and

Who your enemies are."

"Let your family be your best friend."
But understand that they are not perfect.
Sometimes you will have to let them go and
when things settle down you can let them
back into your life with baby steps.
At times you have to keep them
at arm's length.

"Life is all experiences."

Which you must pass through. Without experiences you cannot grow. Let life pass through you and gain all the knowledge.

"All ups must come down.

Patience is a gift

Patience sees you through challenges

Patience brings peace

Patience is inner peace."

"Wherever the art of Medicine is loved,

there is also a love of Humanity."

– Hippocrates

"Encouraging words are good medicine for the soul."

– Lailah Gifty Akita

"A little humility and laughter in our life is good medicine for us! Especially at our own expense! This is how we grow! This is how our spirit survives with essence!"

– Angie Karan Krezos

"Nature itself, is the best medicine prescription, for our whole being."

– Angie Karan Krezos

"The best cure for the body is a quiet mind."

-Napoleon I (1769-1821)

"Painting is silent poetry, and is painting that speaks."

-Plutarch

"Keep your eyes on the stars, and your feet on the ground."

-Theodore Roosevelt

"Life is a journey and only those who connect and cling with the sovereign God will triumph. God does not change nor fail. Be still and know that I am God…"

-Psalm 46 vs 10

"By failing to prepare, you are preparing to fail."

-Benjamin Franklin

"The key is to keep company only with

people who uplift you

whose presence calls forth your best."

-Epictetus

"Things do not happen. Things are made to happen."

-John F. Kennedy

"The harder the conflict, the more glorious

the triumph."

-Thomas Paine

"Do something wonderful, people may imitate it."

-Albert Schweitzer

"The will to succeed is important, but what's more important is the will to prepare."

-Bobby Knight

"The people who influence you are the people who believe in you."

-Henry Drummond

"Put your heart, mind and soul into even

your smallest acts.

This is the secret of success."

-Swami Sivamanda

"It is always the simple that produces the marvelous."

-Amelia Barr

"What we need is more people who specialize in the impossible."

-Theodore Roethke

"Either I will find a way, or I will make one."

-Philip Sidney

"Problems are not signs, they are guidelines."
-Robert H. Schuller

"It does not matter how slowly you go as long as you do not stop."

-Confucius

"Optimism is the faith that leads to achievement. Nothing can be done without hope and confidence."

-Helen Keller

"Quality is not an act, it is a habit."

-Aristotle

"What you do today can improve all your tomorrows."

-Ralph Marston

"The most effective way to do it,

is to do it."

-Amelia Earhart

"True happiness involves the full use of one's power and talents."

-John W Gardner

"Knowing is not enough; We must do."

- Johann Wolgang von Goethe

"You need to overcome the tug of people against you as you reach for high goals."

-George S. Patton

"Believe you can and you're halfway there."

-Theodore Roosevelt

"Enthusiasm moves the world."

-Arthur Balfour

"You must do the things you think you cannot."

-Eleanor Roosevelt

"What we achieve inwardly will change

outer reality."

-Plutarch

"We must let go of the life we have planned, so as to accept the one that is waiting for us."

-Joseph Campbell

"The fate of love is that it always seems too little or too much."

-Amelia Barr

"Great thoughts come from the heart."

-Luc de Clapier

"If you can dream it, you can do it."

-Walt Disney

"The secret of getting ahead is getting started."

-Mark Twain

"In order to succeed, we must first believe that we can."

-Nikos Kazantzakis

"Motivation will almost always beat mere talent."

-Norman Ralph Augustine

"When God Has blessed you,
No one born of a human being can take
that away from you."

"Always sing your own praises, because nobody will do it for you."

"Having a job is great, but striving for your potential is the best."

"Medicine has taught me to be calm, no matter what is around me."

"Life will torment you

Life will drag you down

Life will make you think there is no way

But stand firm and you will see the light."

"As you climb the ladder of success, your friends will fall off because a lot of them don't agree with your vision and its ok. Always look up to God, believe in Him, and trust Him with all your heart. I have never seen where God defeated Himself."

"No one is born with money.

You can inherit it,

You can work hard for it,

You can win the lottery

But know that it does not bring you

happiness;

Happiness comes from you."

"Life is worth living.

You might walk through long corridors,

You might have to be redirected like a GPS,

But you will get your reward."

"Marriage is a journey;

It's not perfect;

You will have good days and bad days;

You will have spiritual fights;

At the end of the day it is a beautiful thing

to vent to someone and grow with

someone."

"Death is imminent.

You should not be afraid of it.

Embrace it and enjoy your journey until

your day is called."

"Co-workers are great.
Learn to keep your life private,
Because you don't want a village in your life."

"Life is what you make of it.

Live it to the fullest,

Love to the fullest;

Climb the highest mountain of your

happiness."

"Remember that only you can make

you happy.

Not even your spouse or lover can make

you happy.

Learn to be by yourself and appreciate the

YOU!"

"Self-satisfaction comes from within.
Study the YOU and bring yourself to light
to enjoy the inner peace of YOU.
Always remember that you are the most
important person on this earth and
everything revolves around you.
From that point you will be able to help the
next person."

"Life is a journey of the unexpected.

Life is not certain so

Enjoy the present."

"Always believe in yourself

No one will do it for you."

"Don't pretend with love.
When you love someone the love will always prevail."

ASL Index	Page
C	
Challenges	1,25,42, 62,74,77,78,81,84
Children/Kids	17, 20, 32, 33, 78
D	
Death	24, 133
Dignity	14
Divorce	12
Dreams	7, 29, 37,54, 59, 64, 120
E	
Emotions	30
F	
Failure	3, 4, 38, 49, 62

Faith	5, 15, 26, 57, 106
Fears	23, 63
Friends	9, 13, 18, 35, 36, 50, 81, 82, 129

ASL Index	**Page**
G	
Gift	31, 32, 35, 78, 84
I	
Inner You	6, 47, 61, 65, 76
J	
Journey	23, 27, 43, 44, 80, 92, 132, 133, 138
Joy	22, 32, 33
Judge	25
L	

Love	11, 16, 17, 28, 32, 36, 46, 65, 66, 70, 85, 118, 135, 140
M	
Marriage	9, 10, 11, 12, 77, 132
Mistakes	3

ASL Index	Page
N	
Negative, Negativity	13, 50, 60
O	
Over-thinking	48
P	
Patience	84
Peace	22, 28, 56, 84, 137

Persistence	38
Pray	10, 17, 18
R	
Respect	14, 15, 16
S	
Silence	21, 30
Strengths/ weaknesses	39, 80
Success	4, 5, 13, 51, 58, 62, 66, 73, 100, 129
T	
Trust	6, 41, 41, 68
U	
Uncertainties	2, 8

Author: Dr Marga Ngwang , M.D

CEO: Nissi Family Medicine
Clinical Faculty at Morehouse
School of Medicine

Medical Director: Signature
Health Care facilities Buckhead/Tower

Consultant: David's Global Community
Development Corp/ Autism Foundation

www.ingramcontent.com/pod-product-compliance
Lightning Source LLC
LaVergne TN
LVHW051522070426
835507LV00023B/3246